THE DAILY OFFICE

How to Pray with the Book
of Common Prayer

David S. Harvey

Copyright © 2024 David S. Harvey

All rights reserved

No part of this book may be reproduced, or stored in a retrieval system, or transmitted in any form or by any means, electronic, mechanical, photocopying, recording, or otherwise, without express written permission of the publisher.

ISBN-13: 9781234567890
ISBN-10: 1477123456

Cover design by: David S. Harvey
Library of Congress Control Number: 2018675309
Printed in the United States of America

CONTENTS

Title Page
Copyright
Introduction
Praying the Offices   1
The Opening   5
The Confession of Sin   8
The Invitatory and Psalter   10
The Lessons   18
The Prayers   24
The Close of the Office   30
A Note about Time   32
Quick Guides   35
Glossary   39
Further Reading   41
About The Author   43

INTRODUCTION

Just as we live on borrowed breath, it is also true that we pray borrowed prayers. We only learn how to pray by praying prayers we did not write, by praying prayers that did not rise up in us at first.

CHRIS E.W. GREEN

The aim for this little booklet is to be a "how to" guide to praying the Daily Office with a print edition of the 1979 Book of Common Prayer (BCP). This guide aims to help you familiarize with the "geography" of the BCP rather than offer an explanation of the content.

Using a print copy of the BCP can be intimidating. There appear to be multiple choices to make and pages to navigate. This quickly makes the prayerbook seem difficult for the uninitiated and discouraging for those looking to pray with the church and traditions.

The idea of this guide is to compile all the instructions (known as **rubrics**) for the Daily Office in a way that allows you to easily pray the office as intended but without the aid of websites or apps. The hope is that as you familiarize yourself with the offices you will also learn to make sense of the rubrics throughout the BCP.

This book uses the *Rite 2 (Contemporary Language) Daily Morning Prayer* as your primary guide and should allow you to "build" the prayer office using simply your 1979 BCP and a Bible, while also helping you learn to use the BCP in your spiritual formation.

Once you have understood how to navigate the *Morning Prayer* liturgy, those rubrics are broadly the same as those for *Evening Prayer.* There is an Quick Guide outline for both services at the end of this book.

The other Offices of the day in the BCP, *Noon* and *Compline,* are services that don't have the same variations as Morning and Evening. As such, they can be prayed simply from the Liturgy as printed.

Some introductory comments for Morning Prayer are noted in *Concerning the Service* p.74 and for Evening Prayer on p.108 with *Additional Directions* for both beginning on p.141.

PRAYING THE OFFICES

The primary purpose of prayer is not to get God to do what we think God ought to do, but to be properly formed. Toward that end we must not limit our praying to our own improvisational prayers, but also incorporate the wise and well-crafted prayers that have been passed on to us.

BRIAN ZAHND

When you are ready, begin by opening your BCP to the section titled Daily Morning Prayer: Rite Two on p.75 of your prayer book. Each copy of the 1979 BCP, regardless of the size, cover or paper, is printed with the same pagination. This means that p.75 in every 1979 BCP is the beginning of Morning Prayer.

It is a good idea to familiarize yourself with the structure of this section of your prayer book. Eventually, you will remember the structure and then you won't need to read through the **rubrics** each time you use it - you'll just select what is appropriate for each day that you pray. That may seem unlikely right now, but it will happen. Trust me. For now it is also worth having a few bookmarks nearby (some editions of the BCP come with several ribbons for this reason).

You will likely notice that page 75 is largely composed of italic text (in red in some editions) known as **rubrics**. You'll encounter these throughout the BCP. They give instructions for the service, such as, who says what, what we should do, and what posture we are invited to take during this part of the prayer service.

Depending on your Christian tradition or background, it may be a little jarring to see instructions at this level of detail. A priest mentor once told me that a BCP service is a "full-body workout". Although unfamiliar at first, I have come to appreciate prayers that engage more of me than just my brain.

The rubrics are guides. Try not to see them as rules that you can get wrong. Learning to pray with the BCP is a journey and not one you should feel uncomfortable with. So the best advice is probably found in the Anglican maxim used about many of the aspects of liturgical life: *All can, some should, none must.*

Most of these traditions that the rubrics guide us in have depth and purpose that are not always immediately apparent. But a little bit of research (or Googling) into, for example, "why do Anglicans stand for the Creed?" will draw you into the beauty of these rubrics.

However, if there are aspects of the service that you don't wish to participate in just yet, such as the sign of the cross prayer, kneeling, bowing, or something else, it is always ok to simply remain seated. But when you feel ready, even on your own, try standing or kneeling and notice how it changes your perspective on the prayer.

> *The Anglican maxim "All can, some should, none must" is worth remembering during any service in the BCP.*

Prayers For Individuals And Groups

Morning and Evening Prayer are services of the church, so you'll immediately notice that the rubrics assume that multiple people are involved, and that the service is being led by an **officiant**. This does not mean you cannot or should not pray the liturgy alone.

If you, like so many of the church who commit to pray the Offices, are alone, then you are simply going to say all the parts yourself. Both officiant and people.

If you are praying in a group or family setting, but not a formal church service, designate one person as the officiant and they will lead through the liturgy with the rest of the group being the **people**.

THE OPENING

The Liturgical Year...calls us to private and personal reflection on the place of Jesus in the daily exercise of our existence.

JOAN CHITTISTER

As you prepare to pray, on page 75, you will immediately notice a rubric that presents two options for beginning this prayer Office:

> *The Officiant begins the service with one or more of these sentences of Scripture, or with the versicle "Lord, open our lips" on page 80.*

Your first choice is whether or not you will begin the

service with a *Confession of Sin*. This can be another area that newcomers to the liturgical traditions struggle with. Once again, however, there is no need to panic, as even the rubrics in the BCP allow you to begin without the confession. If you are planning to skip it, simply move straight to page 80 where you will find *The Invitatory and Psalter*.

If you are going to pray the confession then you can begin with one of the *Opening Sentences*. These sentences are themed to the **Liturgical Seasons** of the Church Calendar.

If you want to understand this better, an explanation of the Calendar begins on p.15 in your BCP. Furthermore, beginning on page 880 are a series of tables to locate the dates of the liturgical seasons.

> *To find the dates of feasts the rule is that you begin with locating the date of Easter (p.882) and then work out the beginnings of the other seasons from there (p.884). The seasons are easily discovered online too.*

There are six main seasons of the Liturgical Calendar, each with a related seasonal color:

Advent (Purple);

Christmas (White);

Ordinary Time after Epiphany (Green);

Lent (Purple);

Easter (White); and

Ordinary Time after Pentecost (Green).

Having found the correct season, you are now able to choose an opening verse for your Morning Office which will precede the confession. You can choose to read a choice of one, several or all of the seasonal options.

Having done this, you are now ready to pray the *Confession of Sin*. However, the service again offers you a choice with its use of "may be said" in the rubric. If you wish to skip the confession turn to p.80.

THE CONFESSION OF SIN

As soon as wrongful thoughts come into your heart, dash them against Christ and disclose them to your spiritual father.

THE RULE OF ST BENEDICT

The Confession of Sin (p.79-80) reminds us simultaneously that we are in need of forgiveness and that it is always offered to us in Christ.

There is an optional introduction for the officiant, but when praying alone the shorter sentence, beginning "Let us confess..." will suffice.

> *Even when alone, remembering the maxim "All can, some should, none must", you may wish to follow the rubrics on posture, such as kneeling.*

An absolution or pronouncement of forgiveness follows the confession. This is phrased to be delivered by a **priest** or a **bishop**. If a **deacon** or a **lay person** is leading at this person, or praying alone, the rubric instructs you to substitute "us" and "our" for the priestly words of "you" and "your", which gives you this sentence:

> *Almighty God have mercy on us, (+)forgive us all our sins through our Lord Jesus Christ, strengthen us in all goodness, and by the power of the Holy Spirit keep us in eternal life. Amen.*

It is common to see people make the sign of the cross at the point marked (+) in this prayer. A Priest will make the sign towards the congregation in a *Morning* or *Evening Prayer* service.

THE INVITATORY AND PSALTER

Good liturgy welcomes us to the wilderness of beholding God in the unfolding truth of ourselves.

MAGGIE ROSS

This is now the beginning of the worship, p.80, where you are being "invited" to worship God. The Psalms are the primary guides in this journey, hence the title of this part of the service.

This part begins with an initial call and response,

Lord, open our lips.

And our mouths shall proclaim your praise.

Followed then by the phrase known as the "Glory be…" or its Latin title, the *Gloria Patri*. Although not mentioned in the **rubrics** it is common that people will bow their heads here during the first part of the *Gloria Patri* where the Trinity is named.

Invitatory Antiphons

You are now invited to select an **antiphon** appropriate to the season. Antiphons are short chants, traditionally accompanied with music, that are said as a refrain to a Psalm or piece of Scripture.

There are a selection of antiphons on pages 80-82, but the guidance on p.141 reminds you that it is appropriate to use any of the antiphons from pages 43-44 with any of the Invitatory Psalms.

With some of the optional invitatory antiphons you will notice the Alleluia is presented like this: [Alleluia]. This is to allow you to choose whether or not it is seasonally appropriate to say the Alleluia, for example, during Lent when the Church traditionally refrains from saying Alleluia.

Venite or Jubilate

We are now offered a choice of either an *Invitatory Psalm* or an *Opening Canticle.* **Canticles** are either psalm-like songs with biblical lyrics, or portions of the Psalms for use at specific points of a service.

> *The BCP names Psalms and Canticles after their first lines. But often their first lines in Latin!*

The *Venite* (p.82), which is Psalm 95:1-7 (although the whole Psalm can be prayed from p.724, or the traditional language option on p.146), or *Jubilate* (p.82) can be chosen to your preference as both invite us into a time of worship in joy. The only variation offered here is the Canticle *Pascha Nostrum* (p.83) which is a gathering up of some great themes in St Paul's epistles and used during Easter Week, or the full season of Eastertide.

> *Easter week is the week beginning with Resurrection (not to be confused with Holy Week which begins on Palm or Passion Sunday), and Eastertide is the season from Resurrection Sunday through to the Day of Pentecost.*

The Psalm or Psalms Appointed

This is where the variations of your daily prayer start to become more pronounced. We are now invited to say (or sing) the appointed Psalms of the day.

The Psalms are a substantial component of the Prayer Offices. It could be said that we learn to pray by praying the Psalms. To learn and understand how the Psalms are used in the Offices we need to turn elsewhere in our BCP.

If this is the first time you have used the BCP for the Daily Office there are some introductory readings that will be helpful to you. Marking p.84, turn to p.582 and read the introduction to the Psalter. This will help you think about how to use the Psalms as prayers both alone and in a group or congregational setting. This can be helpful if you haven't experienced the Psalms used as public prayer before.

Once you have read about how the Psalter can be used for prayer, turn to p.934 and read the section *Concerning the Daily Office Lectionary*. The term *Psalms Appointed* refers to a variety of "tracks" that can be followed to structure your worship. To be clear, you are not going to be making this choice daily, but rather choosing a track that will guide you for the whole month or even year (or possibly two years!). So, after placing a mark in p.84, turn to the Psalter (p.585).

Choice One: The Thirty Day Cycle

The first "option" for use of the Psalms in your daily prayer is the 30 Day Cycle. This takes you through the entire Psalter in 30 days by dividing the readings up between morning and evening prayers. This was the model preferred by Anglicanism at the time of the Reformation and is preserved in your BCP Psalter. When following this track you can read all the Psalms for that day at one time (if you are only praying one Office daily), split them between Morning and Evening, or spread them throughout the day if you are praying the other Offices too.

The 30 day cycle is designed to begin on the first of the month, but that is only because it is easier to remember where you are reading from. Start whenever you wish.

To use this track turn to p.585. You will notice a rubric which reads *First Day: Morning Prayer* written beneath *Book One*. This the beginning of your *Morning Prayer* reading for January 1, February 1, March 1, etc... You will pray through Psalms 1-5 until, on p.589, you encounter *First Day: Evening Prayer*. Beginning at Psalm 6 and praying through to Psalm 8 on p.592 for your *Evening prayer*. Page 593 then begins *Second Day: Morning Prayer* and so it continues through for 30 days.

The **Cranmer** Tradition left no guidance on what to do on a month of 31 days. By the 1662 edition the tradition developed of simply repeating the Psalms from day 30.

> *The Psalter shall be read through once every Month, as it is there appointed, both for Morning and Evening Prayer. But in February it shall be read only to the twenty-eighth, or twenty-ninth day of the month. And, whereas January, March, May, July, August, October, and December have one-and-thirty days apiece; It is ordered, that the same Psalms shall be read the last day of the said Months, which were read the day before: so that the Psalter may begin again the first day of the next Month ensuing.* (The 1662 Book of Common Prayer)

Recent Anglican tradition has suggested that the Psalms of Ascent (Psalms 120-134) are prayed on day 31 giving you for *Morning Prayer* Psalms 120-127, and for *Evening Prayer* 128-134.

The Sixty Day Cycle: The 2019 ACNA Prayer Book offers a program for praying through the Psalms in a more sedate 60 days. This isn't an option in the 1979 Prayer Book but could be easily replicated due to there being 2 readings per day marked throughout the Psalter to assist in the 30 day cycle. You would simply read one per day in a pattern that you could easily remember.

Choice Two: The Daily Office Lectionary

The second option is the *Daily Office Lectionary* readings. This model will guide you through most of the Psalms in around 7-8 weeks. The Psalms in this format will be slightly more closely linked to the other readings of the day (*We will explain how the Daily Office Lectionary works in the next chapter about* the Lessons). You should note, however, that this format does not approach Psalms sequentially, but rather shuffles around in the Psalter so as to connect the Psalms with the readings for each day. This approach obscures the fact that not all the Psalms are used in this format, some are omitted, some only encountered in part. The advantage, however, is that the Psalms will connect a little better with the other Scripture used in your prayer time.

To use this series of readings, go to p.936 and you will see that the Psalms are listed above the day's other readings separated by a ❖ symbol. The Psalms before the ❖ are for *Morning Prayer* and those after the ❖ are for *Evening Prayer*.

Praying the Psalms

Now that you have located and discovered the *Psalms Appointed* for the day you are ready to pray them. You can simply pray through the Psalms as they are printed, but if you are with one or more people p.582 guides you in some options of ways to pray the Psalms with others – *Responsive* (noting the * marks in the BCP Psalter), *Responsorial*, or *Antiphonal*.

> *Responsive reading is the easiest place to begin with a group. In this approach the officiant prays the first line up to the asterisk (*) and the "people" respond by praying the second half of the verse.*

You may also like to try singing or chanting the Psalms. There are multiple examples and guides available online or in print. It will take some practice, but many people find it an enriching experience.

After the *Psalms Appointed* have been read return to p.84 where you will again sing or say the *Gloria Patri* and prepare for *The Lessons*.

THE LESSONS

All of God can be found in every word of Scripture

DIETRICH BONHOEFFER

The Lessons (p.84) always follow The Psalm or Psalms Appointed. The Lessons is a term referring to the selected Scripture(s) for that service, although the title hints towards what the Scripture is doing. Once again, however, you must return your marker to p.84 and leaf through to Concerning the Daily Office Lectionary on p.934 to find out what to read.

This lectionary for your daily readings is a two-year cycle

starting at at Advent, the beginning of the Christian Liturgical year. So you will find the readings on p.934 divided into Year One and Year Two.

Remember, however, that the *Daily Office* is an invitation to pray "with" the church, even when alone. So the two-year program does not just begin whenever you choose, rather, it is tied to the Lectionary cycles. This means that we, the Church, are all praying the same texts at the same time, not just on Sundays via the *Revised Common Lectionary* (RCL), but also by using the two-year *Daily Office Lectionary* in the BCP. Beautifully this means that due to global time-zones and the *Daily Office Lectionary* the Church can fulfill the instruction to "pray without ceasing" (1 Thessalonians 5:18). Somewhere in the world, while you are sleeping, someone is praying the same *Morning Prayers* and *Lessons* that you will pray when you wake. In prayer we really become, as we confess, a holy catholic Church.

Naturally, this means that a rubric is needed to discover whether this current year is "Year One" or "Year Two". Fortunately, it is straightforward:

> *Year One begins on the First Sunday of Advent preceding odd-numbered years, and Year Two begins on the First Sunday of Advent preceding even-numbered years.*

Therefore, the *Daily Office Lectionary* for Year One begins on the First Sunday of Advent 2024, because it precedes the odd-number year 2025.

Beginning then on p.936 the Year One and Year Two *Lessons* are presented on facing pages - so pay attention to the title at the bottom of each page. Rather than presenting the readings sequentially (Year One and then Year Two), the readings for each week are opposite each other. So, for example, Advent 1 Year One is on the page facing Advent 1 Year Two.

You will also notice that there are five readings for each day of each week of the liturgical year. The readings are divided into two sets of Psalms (divided by a ❖ symbol) for *Morning Prayer* and *Evening Prayer*, then on the following line, three more readings; an Old Testament, New Testament, and Gospel.

The introduction on p.934 suggests that the format to use for these three other readings is, two in the morning and one at evening, with the Gospel being used in the morning of Year One and the evening of Year Two. If two readings are preferred at each service, then the Old Testament reading from the alternate year should be used. Alternatively, if you are only praying one Office each day, all the readings should be done at that office (with p.84 reminding you that the Gospel reading is then the final reading).

And so it follows every day throughout the two-year cycle.

Almost. Unless it is a *Holy Day*.

If it is a *Holy Day* then a different set of lectionary texts are used that day. Helpfully it is essentially the same format, you just need to look up the *Holy Days* in their own lectionary area at the very end of the BCP, p.996-1001. These texts are then read for the *Holy Day* before returning to the ordinary lectionary readings for the next day.

It may interest you to know that were you to read all the readings in the *Daily Office Lectionary* over the whole two-year period you would have read something from 37 of the 39 books of the Old Testament (only 1 & 2 Chronicles are missed – largely due to their similarity to 1 & 2 Kings), all 27 New Testament books, and also a few sections of the deuterocanonical Baruch, 1st Maccabees, and the Wisdom of Solomon.

Although the *Daily Office Lectionary* readings are selective, the coverage looks something like this:

New Testament: 100% of Matthew and Mark, 96% of Luke, 91% of John, 100% of Acts, Hebrews, and Revelation, 97% of both the Pauline Corpus and the General Epistles.

Old Testament: Year One reads through about 22% of the OT with more emphasis on history and the Major Prophets. Year Two reads about 25% and focussing more on the Wisdom traditions, the Minor Prophets, and the Law. In total about 47% of the OT is read.

Now that you have gathered your readings for the service, but before reading them, return to p.84 for further instructions regarding what to read along with the day's Scriptures.

The Canticles

Arriving again at p.84, the rubrics inform you that each of the readings (not including the Psalms) are to be followed by a **versicle** and response (e.g. "The Word of the Lord" then, "Thanks be to God"), a silence, and then a choice of **Canticle** before the next Lesson is said.

The options for canticle readings are found in two different locations of your BCP:
    Canticles 1-7 are found on pages 47-52; and,
    Canticles 8-21 are located on pages 85-96.
But how do you choose which Canticle to use?

While this decision is yours, or the leader's, the BCP does help by providing a *Table of Suggested Canticles* for *Morning Prayer* at p.144. Following this allows you to cycle through the Canticles at a rate sufficient to allow familiarity, but infrequent enough to not become dry.

There are minor variations within this table for some of the liturgical seasons, so it is worth paying attention whenever the season changes.

The Apostles' Creed

Continuing and concluding the response to Scripture, after the final canticle of *The Lessons*, *The Apostles' Creed* is said. It is located on p.96.

> *You may notice that some people will bow during the line "He was conceived by the power of the Holy Spirit and born of the Virgin Mary." Others will also make the sign of the cross at the line "the resurrection of the Body."*

THE PRAYERS

I pray because I can't help myself. I pray because I'm helpless. I pray because the need flows out of me all the time, waking and sleeping. It doesn't change God. It changes me.

C.S. LEWIS

From confession, to worship, and then to lessons, now the service arrives at p.97 and a section simply called The Prayers. The first part of which is actually composed of three prayers; a well-known introductory versicle and response, the Our Father, and the Suffrages (which are a sequence of responses composed of lines from Scripture).

Once again there are choices. You can choose between the traditional or contemporary version of the *Lord's Prayer*, and whether you want to pray *Suffrage* A or B. These choices are offered without any further guidance, it is simply a matter of your preference.

The Collects

That small group of prayers are then followed by a selection of prayers known as **Collects** on p.98. There is a substantial debate in liturgics about what "makes a collect a collect", but it will suffice to say here that it is a generally short, thematically appropriate prayer that often only asks one thing of God.

As should be familiar now, you are presented with options of collects to choose from. The **rubric** offers the option of "one or more". One is considered enough however, although many choose to add at least a collect for mission.

The *Collect of the Day* is the collect from the Sunday of that week (unless there is a *Holy Day* or some other day to be observed. That list begins on p.211). The exception to this is Saturday Evening when the Collect for the following Sunday is to be used.

The list of *Seasonal Collects* is found on p.211-236. Simply choose the collect that matches the current week. It may be helpful to note that the week's title in the *Daily Office Lectionary* will match the title in this *Collects* section.

❖ ❖ ❖

The Great Litany

Following the Collects there is a tradition that includes *The Great Litany* in the service here. This is not explained in the rubrics here but rather on p.148. It is at your discretion whether or not you include it. If you choose not to, jump down to the next section *Intercessions and Thanksgivings*.

The Great Litany can be used at Eucharist, or on its own during Lent and Rogation days, or after the collects at Morning and Evening prayers. If you want to include it in your prayers, turn to page 148 before moving on to the *Intercessions*.

You should, however, note that by page 153 of *The Great Litany* there are several options as to how to conclude depending on the service you are including it in.

When using *The Great Litany* in the *Daily Offices* there are a few variations that need your attention. Firstly, following the advice on p.142, you omit the *Our Father* that preceded the Suffrages and Collects. Secondly, you have to decide how you are going to conclude the litany and service. There are essentially three options for this:

1) Follow *The Great Litany* to the "grace" at the top of p.154 and conclude the service there.

2) Follow *The Great Litany* to the "Amen" at the end of the Lord's Prayer on p.153, then turn immediately to p.154 and pray *The Supplication* through to p.155 and conclude the service there.

3) As #2, follow *The Great Litany* to the "Amen" at the end of the Lord's Prayer on p.153, turn immediately to p.154 and follow *The Supplication* through to p.155, but then return to p.101 (For Evening p.125) and continue as usual.

You may find *The Great Litany* beneficial to include at significant times - such as the start of Advent or Lent.

◆ ◆ ◆

Intercessions And Thanksgivings

After the collects, and for the first time in this prayer service, on p.101 there is no script for what to do next. The **rubric** simply offers the option of a hymn or anthem and then "intercessions and thanksgivings may follow". Essentially, this is a pace unscripted prayer.

We should note that while extemporaneous prayer is encouraged by the *Morning Prayer* liturgy, bt it follows after the prayers of the church and the reading of scripture. This functions to "teach us how to pray" so that even our "free prayers" are being shaped and guided by the prayers of the Church as we turn to that which concerns us.

> *What can you pray for here? In short, whatever you want. For others, the lost, the hurt, the dying, or the oppressed. For your family, friends, enemies, and neighbours. The list could be long and all are appropriate. It is, intentionally, unscripted. Which also means it can be as long or short as you want.*

In a group setting the officiant may find it helpful to ask, "For whom or what should we pray?" after which people can simply name that for which they are concerned. After naming it they, or the **Officiant** can say "Lord in your mercy," to which the **People** respond, "Hear our prayer".

This reminds us that in the Church our individual prayers and concerns become the prayers and concerns of the church.

THE CLOSE OF THE OFFICE

You cannot fail at prayer, except by giving it up altogether.

TISH HARRISON WARREN

The Office is now drawing to a close and there are no more page jumps or complex rubrics to navigate. After the extemporaneous prayers everyone unites around either one or both of the General Thanksgiving (p.101) and A Prayer of St. Chrysostom (p.102).

Following this a versicle and response to "Bless the Lord"

is offered (with additional instructions for Eastertide) and then your final choice of one of three Scripture verses that bring the service to a close.

Your prayer time is done. You may go into your day.

Thanks be to God.

A NOTE ABOUT TIME

To worship the Lord is—in the world's eyes—a waste of time. It is, indeed, a royal waste of time, but a waste nonetheless. By engaging in it, we don't accomplish anything useful in our society's terms. Worship ought not to be construed in a utilitarian way...the entire reason for our worship is that God deserves it.

MARVA DAWN

There are an increasing number of resources being created that make it entirely unnessary to even need a little book like this. Excellent apps that will do all the "leafing" through the BCP for you so that every day you just open your device and all the Psalms, canticles, antiphons and readings are correct and ready for you.

None of these are a bad thing. They have helped and continue to help many of us pray with the traditions of the Church - and join the Church each day in prayer.

However, there is something to be said for taking the time away from your digital devices (and their easy interruptions) and finding an unplugged place to pray. But this is not simply an "anti-technology" approach, rather, we should not underestimate the formation that is happening in just taking the time to intentionally organize your prayer time. All that time leafing backwards and forwards is not only slowing you down from the rush of life, but it is also bringing an intentionality to you which will help you be present to the prayers you are about to pray.

Being familiar with your BCP is a helpful skill as well. So try not to consider praying with a real book, away from digital interruptions, as a waste of time that could be done more efficiently. Or perhaps, thinking of the counsel of Marva Dawn, do consider it a waste of time – but that's the point, to know that "wasting time" in the presence of our Heavenly Father is exactly what we should be doing!

When you first start praying the Daily Office from a print copy of the BCP you may find it takes you nearly an hour with all the leafing and searching. Be kind to yourself as you learn. Perhaps read the shorter option of Lessons or choose fewer collects as you find your way.

However, with some practice, a few bookmarks, and a little familiarity you will find that mastering your way around the BCP is not as hard as expected and eventually praying this liturgy will take only 20-25 minutes.

Of course, familiarity with the liturgy does not mean you need to rush the liturgy. But you already knew that.

QUICK GUIDES

On the following pages are the basic outlines, without explanation, to help you build either a *Morning Prayer* or *Evening Prayer* liturgy each day.

This book has not given detailed instructions on Evening Prayer because it essentially follows the same pattern as the Morning Office. So familiarity with one translates easily to the other. However, this quick guide will also help you to navigate.

The outlines simply list the part of the service with the relevant page numbers in the BCP.

Quick Guide: Morning Office

Concerning the Service - p.74 (& p.141)
The Opening - p.75
    Opening Sentences - p.75-78
    Confession of Sin - p.79-80
The Invitatory and Psalter - p.80
    Antiphons - p.80-82 (or p.43-44)
    Invitatory Psalm or Canticle - p.82-83
    The Psalms Appointed - p.84
        30 Day Cycle (using the Psalter's headings) - p.585
        The Daily Office Lectionary - p.936
The Lessons - p.84
    Daily Office Lectionary - p.936
    Canticles - p.84-96 (or p.47-52)
        Table of Suggested Canticles - p.144
    The Apostles' Creed - p.96
The Prayers - p.97
    The *Our Father* and Suffrages - p.97
    Collect of the Day or Seasonal Collect - p.211-236
    General Collects - p.98-101
    Extemporaneous Prayers - p.101
    General Thanksgivings - p.101
The Close of the Office - p.102

Quick Guide: Evening Office

Concerning the Service - p.108 (& p.141)
The Opening - p.115
    Opening Sentences - p.115-116 (or p.75-78)
      or The Service of Light - p.109-112
    Confession of Sin - p.116-117
The Invitatory and Psalter - p.117
    Canticle - p.118 (or Invitatory Psalm - p.82-83)
    The Psalms Appointed - p.118
      30 Day Cycle (using the Psalter's headings) - p.585
      The Daily Office Lectionary - p.936
The Lessons - p.118
    Daily Office Lectionary - p.936
    Canticles - p.119-120 (or p.47-52 or p.84-96)
      Table of Suggested Canticles - p.145
    The Apostles' Creed - p.120
The Prayers - p.121
    The *Our Father* and Suffrages - p.121
    Collect of the Day or Seasonal Collect - p.211-236
    General Collects - p.123-125
    Extemporaneous Prayers - p.125
    General Thanksgivings - p.125-126
The Close of the Office - p.126

GLOSSARY

Antiphon: A short sentence sung or said before or after a Psalm or Canticle.

Canticle: a hymn or chant, composed of biblical texts.

Clergy: **Bishops**, **Priests**, and **Deacons**. These are the ordained ministries of the church. For the purposes of the Daily Office the only substantive difference is that Bishops and Priests can pronounce blessings and absolutions on a congregation (e.g. "May the Lord bless *you*"). Deacons (and lay leaders) will acknowledge the Lord's blessing (e.g. "Almighty God have mercy on us").

Collect: A short prayer, generally one with a singular purpose, often seasonal, that "collects" up the content of the service.

Cranmer: The Archbishop of Canterbury who is largely responsible for the creation of the BCP in 1549.

Lay People: Baptised people of the church who are not in Holy Orders, or Ordained (see *Clergy* above).

Liturgical Season: One of the six liturgical season of the Church Calendar: Advent, Christmas, Ordinary Time after Epiphany (Sometimes known as Epiphany), Lent, Easter, and Ordinary Time after Pentecost.

Officiant: The leader of the liturgy.

People: Any congregation in a liturgy.

Rubric: From the Latin for "red chalk" these are guidance and instructions written within a liturgy.

Versicle: Short sentences, often followed by a congregational response, which are said or sung by the leader of the liturgy.

FURTHER READING

A Glossary of Terms: www.episcopalchurch.org/glossary/

Robert Benson, *In Constant Prayer (Ancient Practices)*, Zondervan, 2010

Alan Jacobs, *The Book of Common Prayer: A Biography (Lives of Great Religious Books)*, Princeton University Press, 2013

Derek Olson, *Inwardly Digest: The Prayer Book as Guide to a Spiritual Life*, Forward Movement, 2016

ABOUT THE AUTHOR

Rev. Dr. David S. Harvey

David S. Harvey is the Director of the St. Anthony Institute for Theology, Philosophy, and Liturgics.

He is ordained as a priest in the Diocese of St. Anthony and pastors at Westside King's Church in Calgary, Alberta.

David taught New Testament at Mattersey Hall College in the UK for many years and received a doctorate in Pauline Studies from the University of Manchester.

He also co-hosts the Two Texts podcast.

Raised in the Pentecostal tradition, David knows what it is to be unfamiliar with traditions such as the Daily Office, and hopes that this book will make the journey easier for you.

The Order of St Anthony is an ecumenical, neo-monastic expression that seeks to provide an ordered way of life for both clergy and laity for prayer, spiritual direction, confession, and spiritual friendship, as well as community. To explore the order visit: www.orderofstanthony.com

The Diocese of St Anthony is called to ordain deacons and priests into Holy Orders, equip affiliated churches, and plant local parishes. To learn more about the Diocese and Holy Orders, visit: www.dioceseofstanthony.com

The St. Anthony Institute is a learning community within the Diocese of St Anthony. Open to all learners, our purpose is to support the formation of those exploring the ordered way of life encouraged within the Order of St Anthony, and the training of those preparing for Holy Orders within our Diocese. To explore the available classes or register to study, visit: www.stanthonyinstitute.com

Two Texts is a Bible Podcast hosted by David Harvey and John Andrews. Every two weeks the two friends release two episodes of unscripted conversation on the Bible. Each episode they pick one text to talk about, which invariably leads to them talking about two texts and often many more. Learn more at www.twotexts.com

Made in the USA
Columbia, SC
08 January 2025